Mastering Google Keep
The Unofficial Guide to Organizing Your Life with Google Keep - Mobile App & Web Edition (Plus 10 Ideas for Getting Started)

By: Rob Ainbinder
http://www.robainbinder.com/books/

Copyright © 2015 Rob Ainbinder. All rights reserved. No part of this book may be reproduced in any form without permission in writing from the author. Reviewers may quote brief passages in reviews.

Disclaimer

No part of this publication may be reproduced or transmitted in any form or by any means, mechanical or electronic, including photocopying or recording, or by any information storage and retrieval system, or transmitted by email without permission in writing from the publisher.
While all attempts have been made to verify the information provided in this publication, neither the author nor the publisher assumes any responsibility for errors, omissions, or contrary interpretations of the subject matter herein.
This book is for entertainment purposes only. The views expressed are those of the author alone, and should not be taken as expert instruction or commands. The reader is responsible for his or her own actions.
Adherence to all applicable laws and regulations, including international, federal, state, and local governing professional licensing, business practices, advertising, and all other aspects of doing business in the US, Canada, or any other jurisdiction is the sole responsibility of the purchaser or reader.
Neither the author nor the publisher assumes any responsibility or liability whatsoever on the behalf of the purchaser or reader of these

materials. Any perceived slight of any individual or organization is purely unintentional.

Your Free Gift

As a way of saying thank you for your purchase, I'm offering a free report that's exclusive to my book readers. With the *Mastering Google Drive Quick Start Guide*, you'll discover a printable reference guide of labels, shortcuts and checklists you'll need to immediately use the full power of Google Keep. Access the free gift at: http://www.robainbinder.com/books/mastering-google-keep

Why Google Keep is Important

Are you constantly looking for a pad of paper, back of a receipt or envelope for the next shopping trip or, to document some part for an auto or, home repair? And, often when you get to the store with the list you may have struggled to translate that written checklist into buying the correct part or, items? Or, worse you misplaced the list. Google Keep to the rescue! If Post-It notes and to-do lists are what you use to help keep the daily chaos at bay, then Google Keep will help even more. Paper lists and sticky notes are replaced by the Google Keep smartphone app and accessible website. Pressed for time? Record a voice memo and Google Keep will transcribe it into a note. With Google Keep the file cabinets of lists of yesterday become obsolete and the chatter from social media, radio and TV are less of a distraction from getting the things you urgently need done.

What is Google Keep? (and Three Reasons to Use Google Keep)

Google Keep is a note taking, checklist and reminder service all rolled into one. You can write notes and checklists on your smartphone app (Android and iOS). So that you will never misplace a note or, the stuff you create in Google Keep is seamlessly synced from/to the Google Keep and Google Keep on the web. More importantly, Google Keep is a powerful organization tool for your life.

Why should you use Google Keep?
1. **Google Keep is free.** There are no Pro plans or, fees to buy the mobile app or, fees to use the web version.
2. **Google Keep is easy to use.** On the web or, in the smartphone app the menus are straightforward and clear. And the information is always on the web and mobile app.

3. **Google Keep is simple.** Many organizational programs are bloated with extra features that only a few users actually use. Google Keep has kept features to a minimum making the menus clear and simple.

Google Keep Basics: What's Included?

Google Keep has lots of great features built in to take your personal productivity to a new level. We'll cover the basic features of Google Keep in this section.

On the Web

The Google Keep taskbar on the web displays at the top of your browser. The icons which display are explained below.

Search Box

At the very top of the screen is a search box. Use the search box to search all notes.

Main Taskbar

On the left is a main menu icon which expands a menu on the left side of the screen.

On the right side is a "refresh" icon and view switching icon. Note: as the browser window is resized (narrower) the view switching icon disappears.

The Google Keep taskbar has the following items:

To access the main menu: click the **menu icon**
Want to learn more about the main menu? Click here.

To refresh the current notes view: click the **refresh icon**

To switch the notes view: click for **grid/list view icon**

Add Note Taskbar

The "Add note" taskbar is where most of the action happens with Google Keep on the web. You can start your note, checklist and photo notes from the "Add note" taskbar.

The "Add note" taskbar in Google Keep web version

- **To add a note**: click "Add note", and begin typing.

- **To create a checklist**: click the **list icon**

- **To create a photo note**: click the **picture icon**

On the Mobile App

The Google Keep Notes taskbar at the top of the mobile app displays a main menu icon, search icon and icon to switch the view.

Main Taskbar

Google Keep main taskbar in Google Keep Mobile App

The Google Keep Notes taskbar has the following items:

- **To access the main menu:** tap the **menu icon**
  Want to learn more about the main menu? Tap here.

- **To search notes:** tap the **search icon**

- **To switch notes view:** tap the **list/grid view icon**

Take a Note Taskbar

The "Take a note.." taskbar appears at the bottom of the app screen. This is where you launch many of the features of the app including taking a note, creating a drawing, recording a voice memo and creating a photo note.

The "Take a note" taskbar in Google Keep Mobile App

The take a note taskbar has the following features:

- **To add a note**: tap in "Take a note..." area and begin typing. To learn more about notes, check here

- **To create a checklist**: tap the **list icon**

- **To create a drawing:** tap the **pen icon**

- **To record a voice memo:** tap the **microphone icon**

- To create a photo note: tap the camera icon . To learn more about photo notes, check here.

Google Keep: Menu Details

Now that you are familiar with the primary menus and functions of Google Keep we will dive into an explanation of the menu available on the Web and in the mobile app.

On the Web

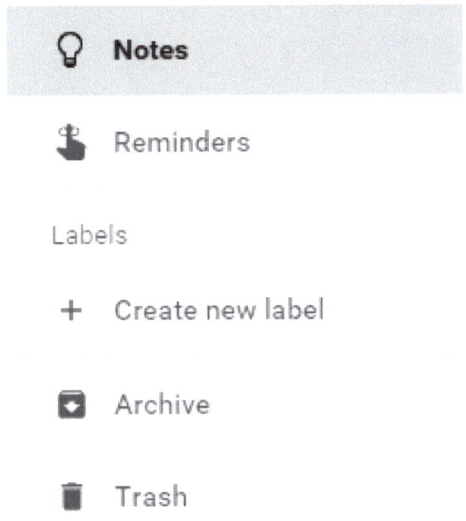

Menu from Google Keep on the Web

To access the menu on the Web follow theses steps.
1. Go to Keep (http://keep.google.com)
2. Click the **menu icon**
3. The main menu displays

The menu on the Web features access to Notes, Reminders, Label creation, Archive access and Trash access.

On the Mobile App

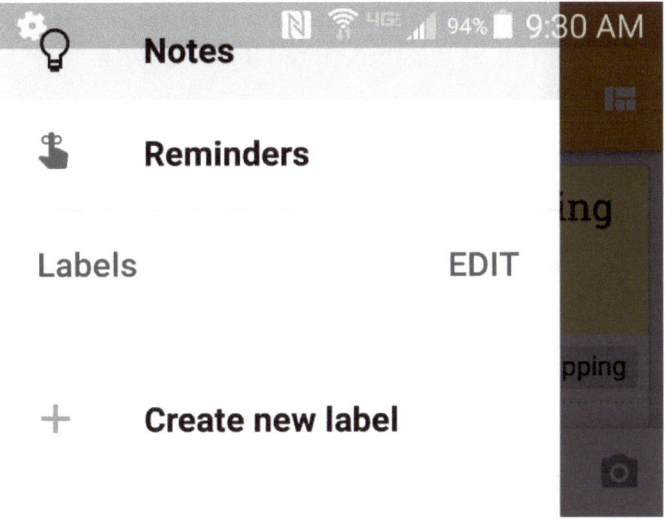

Menu from Google Keep App

To access to menu on the mobile app follow these steps.
1. Open the Keep app
2. At the top of the screen, tap the **menu icon**

The menu on the app features access to Notes, Reminders, Label creation/editing.

Google Keep: Creating Notes

One of the core functions of Google Keep is the creating of Notes. Follow the steps below to write a note in Google Keep.

On the Web

1. Go to Keep (http://keep.google.com)
2. At the top of the page, click **Add note**, then enter your note.
3. To add a title, click **Title**.
4. To save, click **Done**.

On the Mobile App

3. Open the Keep app
4. At the bottom of the screen, tap **Take a note**.
5. To add a title, tap **Title**.
6. To enter text, tap **Note**.
7. To save your note, tap the arrow at the top left.

Google Keep: Coloring Notes

Changing the color of a note can help you visually sort a note based on contents. Or, just color a note for fun! There's no reason all your notes have to be the same color.

The change color picker on Google Keep on the Web

On the Web

1. Go to Keep (http://keep.google.com)
2. If a note isn't open, click on one to edit it.

3. At the bottom of the note, click **Change color**.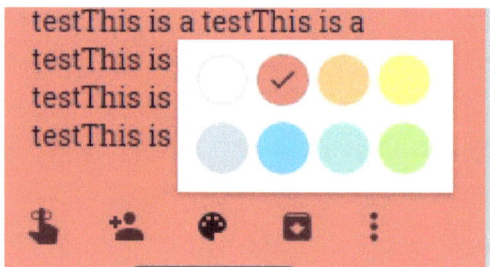
4. Click your color of choice.

On the App

1. Open the Keep app.
2. If a note isn't open, tap one to edit it.

3. At the bottom of the note, tap **Change color**.
4. Tap your color of choice.

Google Keep: Creating Photo Notes

Photo notes add photos from your phone or, computer to your notes. Photos can save you time running back and forth for a project part. Photos can help you make sure you buy the replacement part or, product the first time.

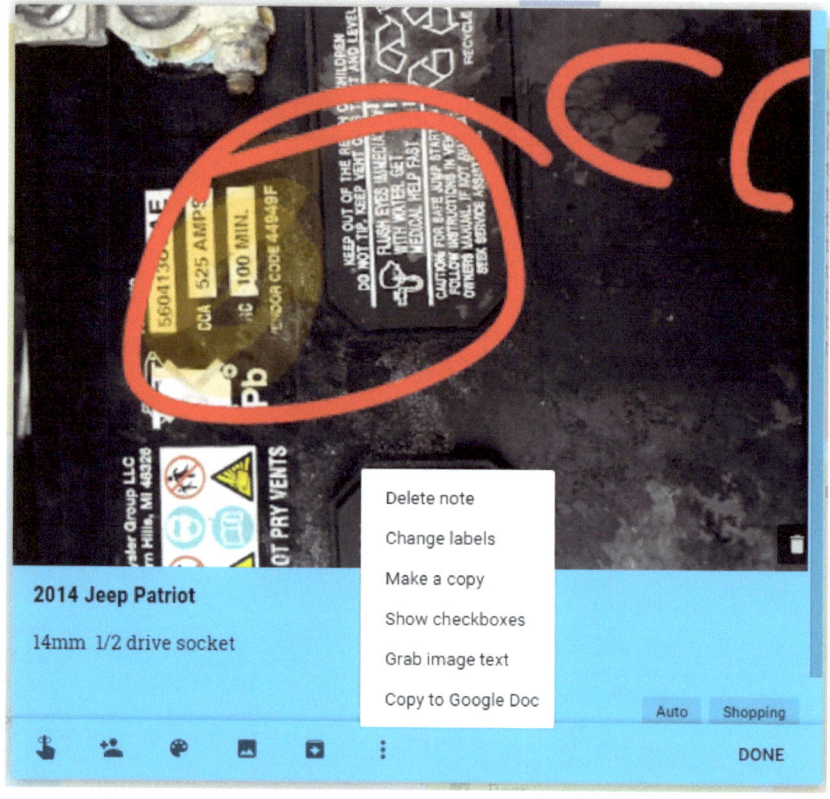

Creating Photo Notes on Google Keep on the Web

On the Web

Creating a Photo Note

1. Go to Keep (http://keep.google.com)
2. Near the top of the page, click the **Add Image icon** .

3. Choose a photo from your computer.
4. To add text, click **Add note**.
5. To add a title, click **Title**.

Adding a photo to an existing note

1. Click the note.
2. Click the **Add Image icon** .
3. Choose a photo from your computer.

To remove a photo: In the bottom right corner of the photo, click the **Trash icon** .

On the Mobile App

Creating a Photo Note

1. On the bottom right of the screen, tap the **Photo icon** .
2. Take a photo or choose an existing image.
3. To enter text, tap **Note**.
4. To add a title, tap Title.
5. To save, tap the **back arrow icon** in the top left .

To remove the photo, tap the **Remove icon** .

Adding a Photo to an Existing Note

1. Tap the note.
2. In the top right, tap the **More icon** .
3. Take a photo or, choose an existing image.

To remove the photo, tap the **Remove icon** on the photo .

Google Keep: Grabbing Image Text

One of Google Keep's most powerful features is its ability to capture text from an image. Load up an image and let Google Keep do the work of transcribing the text from the image.

On the Web

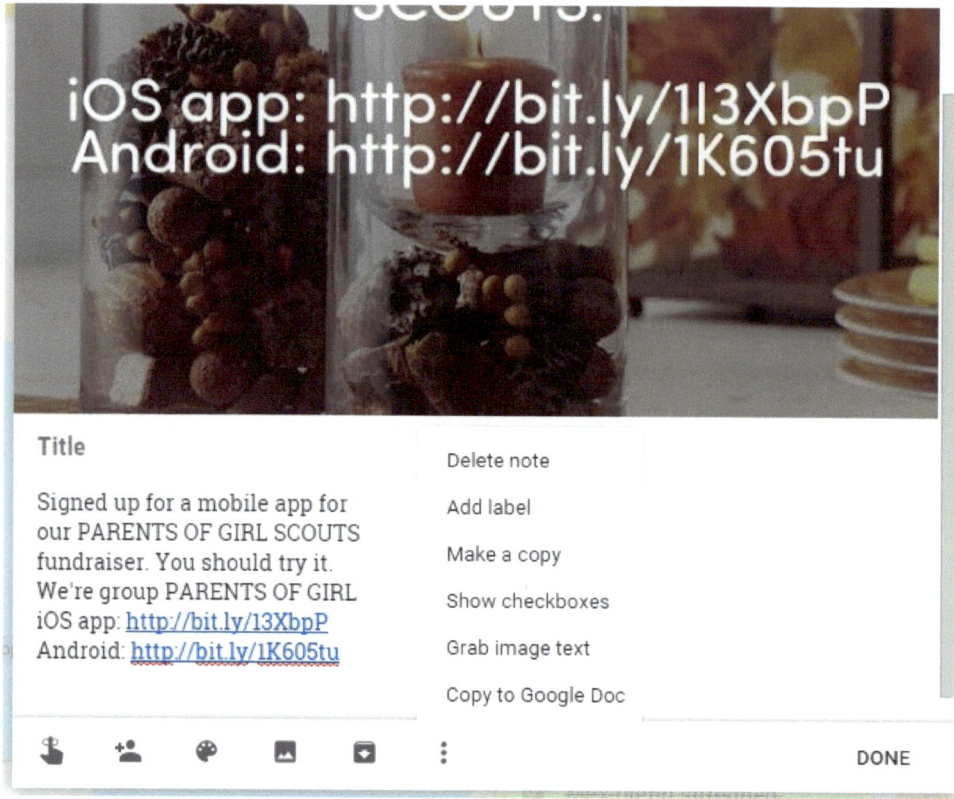

Grabbing text from an image in Google Keep on the Web

1. Go to Keep (http://keep.google.com)
2. Add a Photo to a Note
3. If the photo is already added to the note, Click on the Photo
4. At the bottom of the window, click the **More icon** , click **Grab Image Text**
5. Text from the image is copied to the note area.

6. Edit or, save the note.

On the Mobile App

1. Open the Keep app.
2. Add a Photo to a Note
3. If the photo is already added to the note, tap the photo.
4. The photo opens in a new window.
5. At the bottom of the window, tap the **More icon** ⋮ , tap **Grab Image Text**
6. Text from the image is copied to the note area.
7. Edit or, save the note.

Your Free Gift

As a way of saying thank you for your purchase, I'm offering a free report that's exclusive to my book readers.

With the *Mastering Google Drive Quick Start Guide*, you'll discover a printable reference guide of labels, shortcuts and checklists you'll need to immediately use the full power of Google Keep.

>>> Tap Here to Grab the Master Google Drive Quick Start Guide <<<

Google Keep: Capturing Web/App Content (Mobile App Only)

When you see content you want to capture in a note, follow these steps:

1. At the top right of your device's screen, tap the **More icon** > Share.
2. In some apps, you'll see one of the **Share icons** or or . Tap the **Share icon**.
3. Note: If the app you're using doesn't feature one of these share options, that means you can't create a Keep note from that app. In the iOS app, see In iOS below.
4. Tap Keep. A note will be created that captures the content you're viewing.
5. Optional: Edit your note and add a title.
6. To exit your note: At the top left, tap the back arrow .

In iOS

1. Scroll through the top row of apps, then tap the More icon .
2. To turn on Keep as a sharing option, tap the switch next to Keep. Once you've added Keep, you don't need to add it again.
3. Tap Done.

Google Keep: Creating a Drawing (Mobile App Only)

1. At the bottom right of the screen, tap the **Drawing icon** .
2. Start drawing.

3. To close the drawing, tap the **back arrow icon** in the top left.

Adding a Drawing to an Existing Note

1. Tap the note.
2. In the top right, tap the **More icon** > **Add drawing**.
3. Start drawing.

Using Drawing Tools to Change a Drawing

- Pen
- Marker
- Highlighter
- Eraser. Double-tap the eraser icon or, swipe up on the toolbar to see the "Clear Canvas" button.

Changing the Brush Size or Color

1. Select a brush.
2. To see colors and sizes, tap the brush again or, drag the bottom toolbar up.
3. For more colors, drag up again on the bottom toolbar, or tap the **Expand icon**.

Changing or Editing a Drawing

- **Zoom in**: Move two fingers apart on the canvas.
- **Zoom out**: Pinch two fingers together on the canvas.
- **Pan**: Tap and drag the canvas with two fingers.
- **Undo actions**: Tap **Undo icon** at the top right of the screen.
- **Redo actions**: Tap **Redo icon** at the top right of the screen.

- **Remove the drawing**: Tap the **Remove icon** on the drawing ⊗.

- **Select, move, or resize part of your drawing**:
    - Tap the **Select icon**, then use your finger to select part of your drawing.
    - Pinch or expand with two fingers to scale the selection, or drag with one finger to move it.
    - To see the "Clear Selection" button, tap the **Select icon** or, drag up on the toolbar.

Google Keep: Converting a Note to a List

1. Open a note
2. Click the **More icon** > **Show checkboxes**
3. Google Keep will automatically add a checkbox at the beginning of all line items.

Removing Checkboxes

1. Open a list
2. Click the **More icon** > **Hide checkboxes**
3. Google Keep removes checkboxes at the beginning of all line items.

Tip: Select "Show checkboxes" at the beginning of a new note will automatically trigger Keep to add checkboxes as you add tasks

Google Keep: Copying a Note to Google Drive

Copying a note to Google Drive opens up a number of features including extended text editing and the ability to share this document with collaborators. In addition, you can copy multiple notes and combine them into one new Google Drive document.

On the Web

Copy One or More Notes to a Google Doc

1. Go to Keep (http://keep.google.com)
2. Hover over a note you want to copy, then click the **check mark** . Repeat for any other notes you want to include.
3. In the gray action bar at the top, click the **More icon** > **Copy to Google Doc**.

Copying a Note While It's Open

At the bottom right of the note, click the **More icon** > **Copy to Google Doc**.

At the bottom of your screen, you'll see "Copying to Google Doc". When the Doc is ready, you'll see "Copied to Google Doc". To open the Doc, click **Open**.

On the App

Copying One or More Notes to a Google Doc

1. Open the Keep app.
2. Tap and hold a note you want to copy until it darkens.
3. To include more notes, tap the other notes.
4. At the top right, tap the **More icon** > **Copy to Google Doc**.

Copying a Note While It's Open

At the top right of the note, tap the **More icon** ⋮ > **Copy to Google Doc**.

At the bottom of your screen, you'll see "Copying to Google Doc". When the Doc is ready, you'll see "Copied to Google Doc." To open the Doc, tap **Open**.

Google Keep: Audio Note

Note: Voice Memo recording is a Mobile App only feature. You will not be able to record a voice memo on the web version of Google Keep. Also, if your device is running Android 4.0, you can speak your note but, the recording isn't saved. On the Web you are able to listen to and download an audio note (in .AAC format).

On the App

1. Open the Keep app.
2. At the bottom right, tap the New Audio Note icon 🎤 .
3. Speak your note.
4. When you're done, stop speaking. Your note note will display with the audio file attached below it.
5. To add a title, tap Title and enter your text.
6. To edit the spoken text, tap the text above the audio file.
7. To save your audio note, tap the **back arrow icon** at the top left ← .
8. To remove the recording, tap the Remove icon .

Google Keep: Creating Lists

To create a list in Google Keep follow these steps.

On the Web

1. Go to Keep (http://keep.google.com)
2. Near the top of the page, click the **New list** icon .
3. To create a list item, start typing.
4. To add more list items, click **+ List item**.
5. To add a title, click **Title**.
6. To save your list, click **Done**.

Tip: To reorder a list item, click and hold the item, then move it to your desired location.

On the App

1. Open the Keep app.
2. At the bottom right, tap the **New list** icon .
3. To create a list item, start typing.
4. To add more items, tap **+ List item**.
5. To add a title, tap **Title**.
6. To save your list, tap the **back arrow icon** at the top left .

To remove an item on your list: tap it, then tap **Remove** .
To check and uncheck items on your list: tap the box next to the item.

To hide checkboxes: tap More > **Hide checkboxes**.

Google Keep: Copying a List to Google Drive

On the Web

Copy One or More List to a Google Doc

1. Go to Keep (http://keep.google.com)

2. Hover over a list you want to copy, then click the check mark ✓. Repeat for any other lists you want to include.
3. In the gray action bar at the top, click the **More icon** ⋮ > **Copy to Google Doc**.

Copying a List While It's Open

At the bottom right of the list, click the **More icon** ⋮ > **Copy to Google Doc**.

At the bottom of your screen, you'll see "Copying to Google Doc". When the Doc is ready, you'll see "Copied to Google Doc". To open the Doc, click **Open**.

On the App

Copying One or More Lists to a Google Doc

1. Open the Keep app.
2. Tap and hold a list you want to copy until it darkens.
3. To include more lists, tap the other notes.
4. At the top right, tap the **More icon** ⋮ > **Copy to Google Doc**.

Copying a List While It's Open

At the top right of the list, tap the **More icon** ⋮ > **Copy to Google Doc**.

At the bottom of your screen, you'll see "Copying to Google Doc". When the Doc is ready, you'll see "Copied to Google Doc." To open the Doc, tap **Open**.

Google Keep: Coloring Lists

Changing the color of a note can help you visually sort a note based on contents. Or, just color a note for fun! There's no reason all your notes have to be the same color.

The change color picker on Google Keep on the Web

On the Web

1. Go to Keep (http://keep.google.com)
2. If a list isn't open, click on one to edit it.
3. At the bottom of the list, click **Change color**.
4. Click your color of choice.

On the App

1. Open the Keep app.
2. If a list isn't open, tap one to edit it.

3. At the bottom of the list, tap **Change color**.
4. Tap your color of choice.

Google Keep Automation: Setting & Using Reminders

Setting a Time Based Reminder

On the Web

Set up time reminders on the web to receive a pop-up notification at specific times.

Note: To turn on Keep reminders for the web, you may be prompted to allow browser notifications.

To create a time reminder:

1. While editing a new or existing note, click the **Remind me** icon
2. Choose or enter a date and time.
3. To set up a recurring reminder, click **Does repeat** and choose **daily, weekly, monthly, yearly,** or **custom**.
4. Click **Save**.
5. The reminder will appear at the bottom of the note.

On the App

To receive a reminder a specific time:

1. While editing a new or existing note, tap **Remind me** .
2. To change the default date, tap **Tomorrow**.

3. To change the default time, tap **Morning**.
4. To save, tap the back arrow ← or ✓.
5. You'll see the date and time you've set at the bottom of your note.

Note: When you receive a reminder, you can snooze it or choose to be reminded later.

Setting a Location Based Reminder

The location reminder uses Wifi and/or GPS to notify you when you are near a location that you specify in the note. One practical example of this is: A note of "buy milk" with the location set to the local grocery store. When you get near the grocery store you'll receive a message notification to "buy milk".

On the Web

Note: To get more accurate location reminders, you may be prompted to turn on your computer's location. Click **Allow**.

To create a location reminder:

1. While creating a new note or editing an existing one, click the Remind me icon .
2. Click **Pick place** .
3. Enter the name or address of the location.
4. Click **Save**.

On the App

Note: It's recommended to have Wi-Fi turned on to get more accurate location reminders and conserve battery usage.

To create a location reminder:

1. While editing a new or existing note, tapap **Remind me** .
2. Tap the clock icon .

3. Select **Location reminder**.
4. Enter the name or address of the location.
5. Choose one of the search results.
6. On iOS: tap the checkmark and you'll see the location you've set at the bottom of your note.

Editing & Deleting a Reminder

1. In the top left, select the Menu icon.
2. Select **Reminders**.
3. Open the note you want to edit or delete.
4. To make past reminders appear again, change the time and date of the reminder.
5. To delete a reminder, select the Delete icon.

Searching Google Keep

Google Keep harness search to help you find Notes and other items in Keep in a variety of ways.

The search box in Google Keep on the Web

On the Web

Search filter options display in Google Keep on the Web

To find a note, list, picture or, other item in Keep follow the steps below:

1. Go to Keep (http://keep.google.com)
2. Click in the search box at the top of the window.
3. Search filter options display below the search box.
4. Select one or, more search filters by clicking on them.
5. Enter your search

Search filter options include the following (from left to right):
- Filter by list - filter and display only lists
- Filter by audio - filter and display only audio notes
- Filter by image - filter and display only images
- Filter by reminder - filter and display only reminders
- Filter by shared - filter and display only shared notes/lists
- Filter by color - filter and display only notes/lists with a color applied or, none (no color applied)
    - None
    - Red

- Orange
- Yellow
- Gray
- Blue
- Teal
- Green

On the App

Google Keep search on the Google Keep app.

To find a note, list, picture or, other item in Google Keep app follow the steps below:

1. Open the Keep app.
2. Tap the search icon.
3. Search filter options display below the search box.
4. Select one or, more search filters by tapping them.
5. Enter your search

To add Keep item color to your search

1. Tap the color pallet icon.

2. Tap the color or, colors to include in the search
3. Your view will update and display Keep items matching your choice.

Your Free Gift

As a way of saying thank you for your purchase, I'm offering a free report that's exclusive to my book readers.

With the *Mastering Google Drive Quick Start Guide*, you'll discover a printable reference guide of labels, shortcuts and checklists you'll need to immediately use the full power of Google Keep.

>>> Tap Here to Grab the Master Google Drive Quick Start Guide <<<

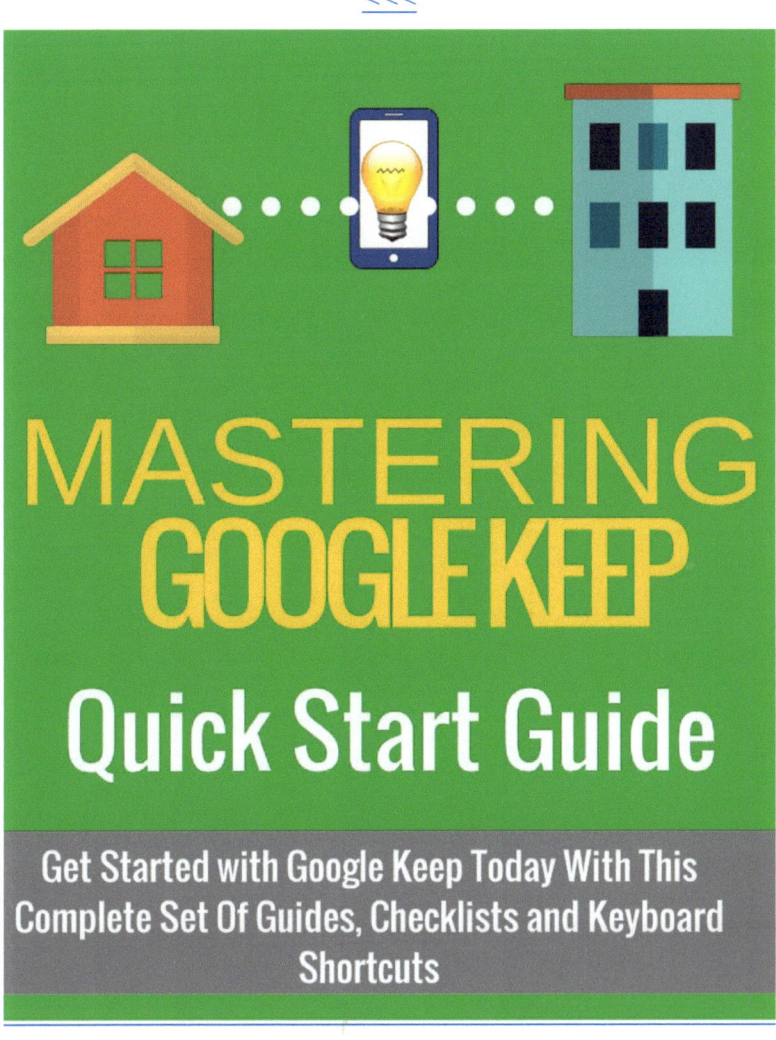

Ways to Organize Your Life with Google Keep

The possibilities of improving your personal productivity with Google Keep are only limited by your imagination. We will discuss two methods: Google Keep labels and the Hashtag/Keywords approach. First, we introduce the fundamentals of Keep labels.

Google Keep: Sorting Notes with Labels

At their core, labels, like those on a folder, help you recognize one label from another. The important twist is that, when you select a label in Google Keep only those notes tagged with a given label appears.

When you select a label your view immediately changes to include only the notes with the selected label. In the below image there is a "Marketing" label applied to the voice memo test note.

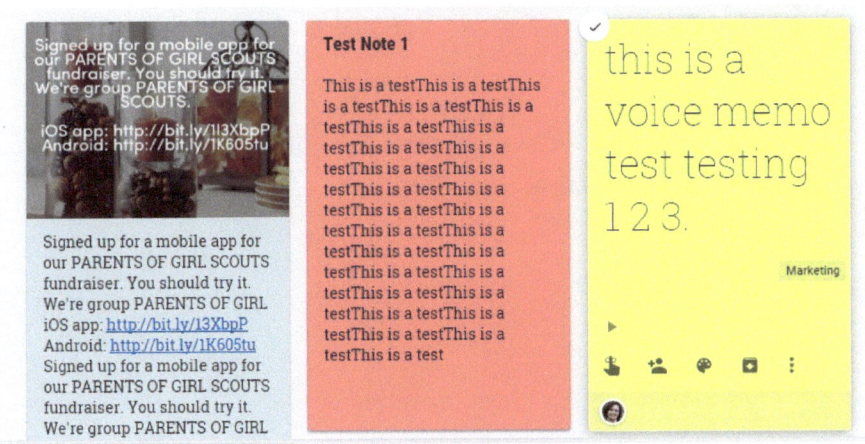

Google Keep: A view of notes without a label sort applied to the view.

When you select a label the view automatically changes to show only the note(s) with the selected label. In the updated screen (below) we have selected the marketing label.

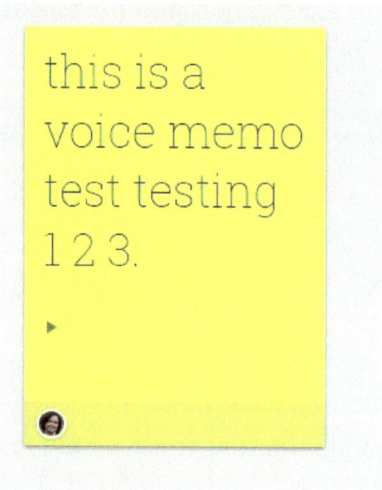

Google Keep with the "marketing" label applied to the view

Using this feature will allow you to have hundreds of notes easily accessible with a click/tap of a label.

On the Web
To sort by a label:
1. Go to Keep (http://keep.google.com)
2. Click the **menu icon**
3. The main menu displays
4. Click the label you'd like to sort on
5. The note view is sorted by the selected label

On the App
To sort by a label:

1. Open the Keep app.
2. Tap the **menu icon** ≡
3. The main menu displays
4. Tap the label you'd like to sort on
5. The note view is sorted by the selected label

Google Keep: Adding & Changing Labels to a Note

On the Web

To add a label to a single note:

1. Go to Keep (http://keep.google.com)
2. Select the note you want to apply the label to.
3. Click the More icon ⋮.
4. Select **Add label**.
5. Either select an existing label or enter a new label name.

To apply the same label to more than one note:

1. Hover over each note you want to apply the label to and click the check mark ✓.
2. In the top action bar, click the More icon ⋮.
3. Select **Change labels**.
4. Either select an existing label or enter a new label name.

To remove or change a label:

1. Choose the note(s), then click the More icon ⋮.
2. Click **Change labels**.
3. Change or remove your labels.

On the App

To add a label to a single note:

1. Open Keep.
2. Choose a note, then tap the Add label icon .
3. Either select an existing label or click "Add label" and type a new label name.
4. To save, click the back arrow .

To remove or change a label:

1. Choose the note(s), then tap the Label icon .
2. Change or remove your labels.

To apply the same label to more than one note:

1. To select more than one note, tap and hold your first note until you see it darken.
2. Tap the other notes you want to include.
3. In the top action bar, tap the Add label icon .
4. Either select an existing label or click "Add label" and enter a new label name.

Hashtags & Search Keywords

Some other ways to organize your notes and lists is through the use of hashtags and search keywords.

Hashtags

With hashtags you would add a keyword with the "#" symbol to the text of your note. For example: *#inspiration* could be used to tag a running list of inspirational quotes. Whenever you wanted to see the inspirational quotes enter the hashtag *#inspiration* into Google Keep's search.

Search Keywords

Using search keywords you would designate a list of keywords to help you manage notes/lists. The idea here, is to use a recurring list of keywords and use them consistently. For example: You might decide to use a combination of your initials and the term as a keyword.

10 Ways to Use Google Keep

1.) Create a shared grocery list (with your husband/wife boy/girlfriend) and set a location based reminder for the local grocery store.
2.) If you're a teacher, designate a color for a certain type of list, for example, use a list color for student assignment/activity ideas.
3.) Use a photo note of your vehicle's oil/air filter and set a reminder for oil/air filter changes.
4.) Are you a blogger? Keep a running list of post ideas.
5.) Are you a writer? Draft a chapter in Google Keep then, copy it to a Google Doc for further development.
6.) Use Keep to track holiday present ideas that occur throughout the year.
7.) Create a note with your husband/wife's sizes/colors.
8.) Track your business mileage in a note by date.
9.) Create a daily checklist with a recurring reminder.
10.) Use a list for a weekly menu and share it with family members.

Troubleshooting Google Keep

For issues with Google Keep check the [official troubleshooting information](#).

Did You Like Mastering Google Keep?

I am genuinely interested in your feedback on the book. It would be of great value to me if you would leave an Amazon review.

More Books by Rob Ainbinder

Want to know when Rob release another book? [Contact him](#).

About Rob Ainbinder

Rob has over 12 years experience in online marketing and strategy in a wide range of industries, including energy, gas, B2B and e-commerce. He is fascinated by all things technology. Rob lives with his family in North Carolina and is the owner of [Why People Click](#).

www.ingramcontent.com/pod-product-compliance
Lightning Source LLC
Chambersburg PA
CBHW040250220526
45473CB00001B/431